bbity-fa
NTS? Ohmygiddygodstrousers!
sity How should I Know? Mucho excitemondo Wha
, questions Fabbity-fab To be or not to be ooo
me of PANTS? Ohmygiddygodstrousers! Question
mosity How should I Know? Mucho excitemondo W
Fabbity-fab To be or not to be ooooo-er Sn
f PANTS? Ohmygiddygodstrousers! Questions, qu
ouser! Snog wisely Wisdomosity How should I Kno
questions, questions, questions Fabbity-fab To be
mondo What in the name of PANTS? Ohmygiddy-
o-er Snog wisely Wisdomosity How should I know
Questions, questions, questions Fabbity-fab To b
temondo What in the name of PANTS? Ohmygidd
ooo-er Snog wisely Wisdomosity How should I Kn
! Questions, ques   Ohmy
o-er Snog wise   ld I kn
citemondo What in the na   ab To
ooooo-er Snog wisely Wisdomosity How should I
rs! Questions, questions, questions Fabbity-fab
              t in the name of PANTS? Ohm
                                 How should

D1420232

Find out more about Georgia at:
www.georgianicolson.com

First published in Great Britain in 2008 by HarperCollins
Children's Books, a division of HarperCollins Publishers Ltd,
77-85 Fulham Palace Road, Hammersmith, London W6 8JB

1 3 5 7 9 10 8 6 4 2

ISBN-13: 978-0-00-728872-4
ISBN-10: 0-00-728872-7

Copyright © Louise Rennison 2008
The author asserts the moral right
to be identified as the author of the work.
All rights reserved.

Printed and bound in China

Georgia Nicolson's Book of Wisdomosity

Louise Rennison

HarperCollins *Children's Books*

Hello Chumettes,

As you know, I am practically Baby Jesus, the Buddha and Mystic Meg all rolled into one. (And no, I do not mean I am a big fat baby wearing a headscarf, you cheeky minxes.) What I mean is that I've decided to share the enormous wisdomosity I have learnt while queuing up at the cakeshop of agony. And hanging around on the rack of luuurve. So when you need an answer to one of life's little problemettes — such as "What in the name of PANTS is wrong with boys?" — simply ask my book. Turn to a page and the answer will appear mysteriously. Like a mirage in the desert. Or a cakey, just when you thought there was no cakey left.

If your question involves a potential snoggee, think through the alphabet while flicking the pages and stop when you get to the first letter of his name. Or perform your finest disco inferno dance, chuck the book in the air (taking care not to knock yourself unconscious) and read the page that it opens on when it lands. Or ask a number to appear in your brainbox and then count to it while turning the pages. Or...

Look, I'm tired now, so get on with it. And I mean that in a loving and caring way.

Georgia X

p.s. Oh, I don't know... get your cat to choose - wherever it puts its paw, there's your answer!

Yes, yes
and thrice
yes!
You know you
want to.

Your
brain
appears
to have gone on
holiday
by mistake.

This is
50
million
hours too
late.

Never eat anything bigger than your head.

Parents
are all the same –
extremely
childish.

Do not
put off till
tomorrow the
snogging
you could do
today.

Is life
over?
Is this all there is?
Or as the Latin folk say,
"Life is-us
a mockery-us
of a sham-us."

Stop looking at it in that lookingy way.

I see a
snog
at the end
of the
tunnel.

It is
vair vair
tiring,
this boy
bananas.

There is **nothing** like shutting the stable door and **tarting up** the horse after it's bolted.

Bigger is better.

(Unless we are talking about noses. Or **nunga-nungas** that become a shelf-like affair that you can balance your snacks on.)

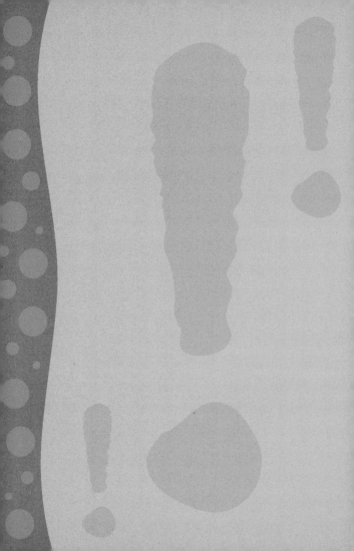

You
cannot
possibly risk going out
**without
make-up
on.**

Boys
are
truly
weird.

(And are you sure he
isn't a secret
Blunder Boy?)

All boys

are mad as snakes – train
yourself up for lesbianism,

even if

it involves growing a

moustache.

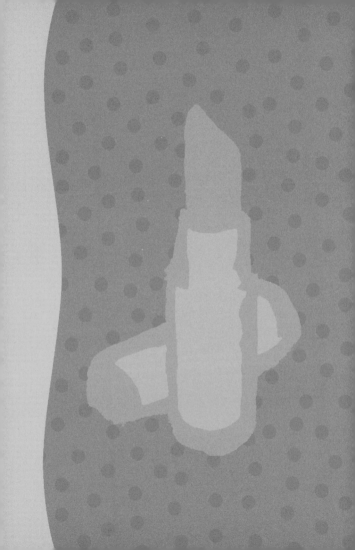

If in doubt, reapply lip gloss for **maximum snognosity.**

Time for a **pore tightening mask** (Because there is **nothing worse** than loose pores.)

The whole thing is a mystery.

Let your
creativitosity
run **wild**
and **free!**

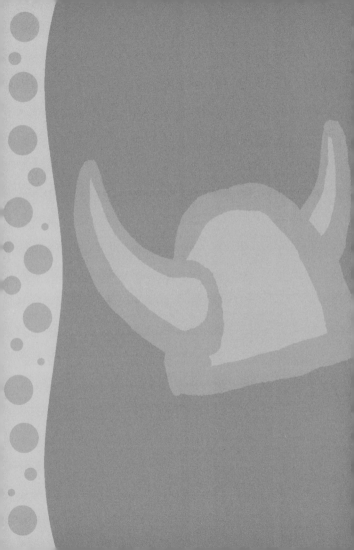

Sound the Cosmic Hoooooorn!

Oh, the old record **plays again;** it's always **you** that does things **wrong.**

Become more
mature quickly –
start
tomorrow.

Boys are **truly** unbelievable. In this case though "s'later" really does mean "see you later".

Use one of your
many
talents...
disco dancing,
for example.

Practise
snogging
makes
perfect
snogging.

Boy entrancers

will not

let you down.

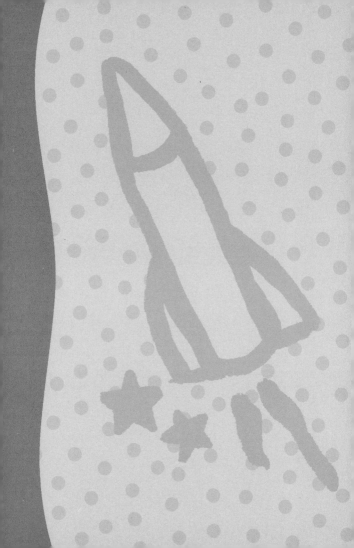

Your
spaceship
has **landed,**
please get in.

You
are half
girl,
half
turnip.

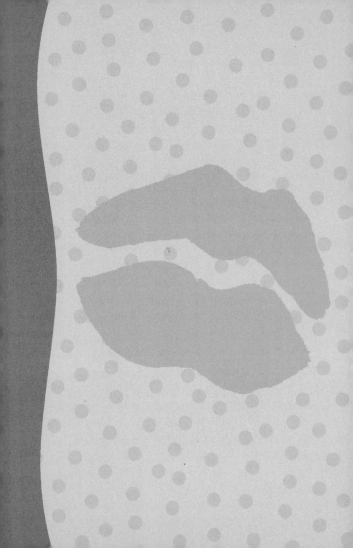

Let your
red-bottomosity
guide the way.

Qu'est-ce que le point?

Dancing in the **nuddy-pants** relieves many tensions.

Prepare for the
unexpected -
the cake shop of
agony may be
closed or it may
be **open...**
So always carry an
emergency snack.

Fate
is a fickle
mistress
or mister, depending on
the way you look at
things.

Seize
the day by its
ginormous
Knickers!

Billy Shakespeare said,
'forsooth'
and **'lack a day'**,
and so should you.

p.s. But do not wear a
beard when you say it.

Writing lists of
reasons
can be helpful.
But it is also
vair vair
boring.

The
mysteries
of
luuurve
will soon be
revealed.

Don't waste your time – it waits for no **man, WOMAN** or **Sex Kitty.**

The **world** is **your**

oyster

which is a shame
because oysters are

whelk-like

and **gross.**

Remove your own obstacles –

break down
the barriers
so you can run

Wild and free.

However don't make a

fool of yourself by

running wild and free in your

nuddy-pants.

A
Luuurve
God
is for life
not just for
Chrimboli.

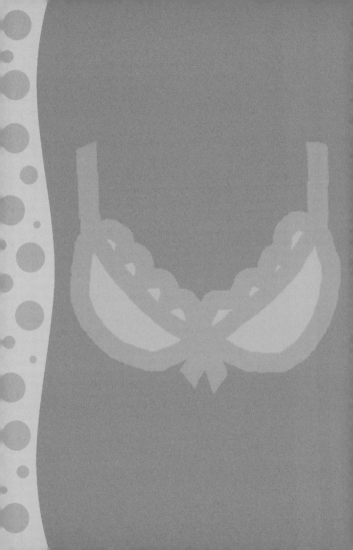

Take a walk on the **wild** side. But not too wild – don't try your Hunchback of Notre Dame impression in public.

The

rack
of love

awaits you.

You are beyond the **Valley** of the **Confused** and treading lightly towards the land of the **Severely Deranged.**

Wakey, wakey,
it's
luuurve
o'clock!

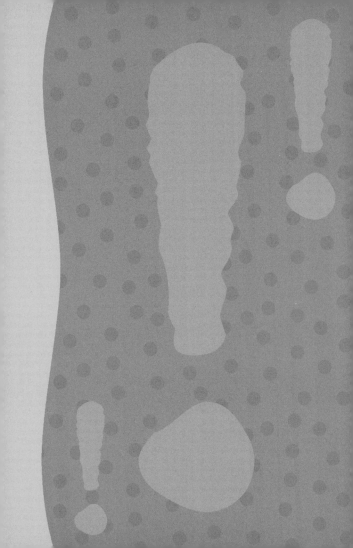

Don't

be ridiculous.

It is

vair
unsophis.

Like

flouncy

shampoo ad girls,

you're worth it.

However don't make the
mistake of telling anyone
as they will hate you.

Seek

and ye shall find.

Unless you can't be

bothered.

in which case there is

no hope for you,

as you are a lazy minx.

Call

Dr Gorgeous

– you've taken one

too many

loon

tablets.

Smile
attractively
and the world **smiles**
with you.
(But make sure

your **nose**

doesn't spread
all over your face.)

Out
with the
old,
in with the new.

Face it,
    you don't

really

        care,

            do you?

A major
boy fiasco
is on the
cards.

Rightio.
Time for
plan B.

Now you **can.** You know you **want to!**

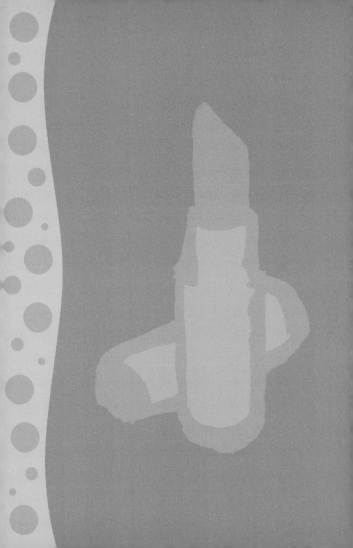

Beauty
is in the eye
of the beholder,
so make sure they are
beholding your best
'natural look'.

Decisions,
decisions,
always more
decisions.

Or something... maybe...
Erm... What do you think?

Let your

nunga-nungas

do the

talking!

A
boy
in the hand
is worth
two
on the bus.

Time to
play the callous
sophisticate.

In this
situation
it is best
to go
shopping.

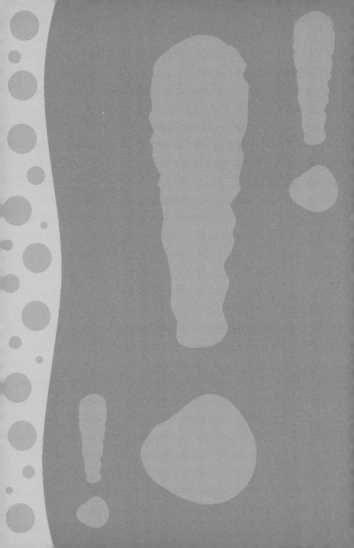

Ohmygiddygodstrousers!

You

are supposed to be

thinking about

make-up and your

nungas-nungas,

Not life-changing

decisions.

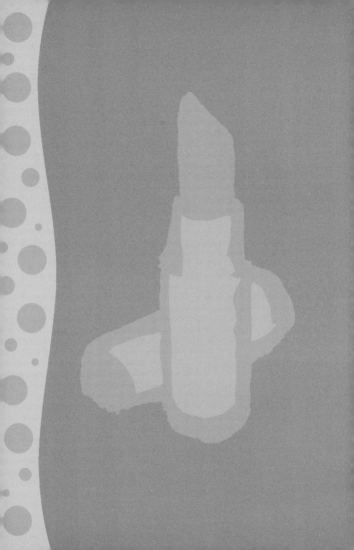

Put on some
mascara,
lippy
and
joie
de vivre.

You can spend the whole afternoon **arguing** about whether you should give it a **second chance.** And **you will still** not know the answer.

Like Angus
in the face of
trouser-snake
addenda removal,
strut your
stuff
with dignitosity at
all times.

Nothing
can alter the
facts.
They have been written in stone
and cannot be **Tippexed**

out unfortunately.

Cross-eyed Gordy has **MORE** sense than you.

Do **not** negotiate. You may be **wrong** but that is part of the **fun!**

When it rains,
it pours.
Especially
when you have not
arranged
your lift
home.

If at first you don't succeed, **snog,** **snog,** and **snog** again!

You are a

BABE
magnet.

Nothing else is
important.

You
will
live to **snog**
another day.

Mucho
excitemondo
and jelloid
Knickers
activity!

You must have done
something
incredibly
bad in a past life.

You are a

bean in
a bikini

tossed on the
sea of life.

Stop

interrupting

yourself, you will only

get more **confused.**

Pardon?

What do
YOU think?
How should you know?
If anyone knows it
won't be you.
You will be the
last to know.

Times are changing.

Relationships are
more complicated.

Maybe you
ARE allowed
two boyfriends
at once...

Act as though it is **already real** but make sure no one knows you are **acting**.

Otherwise you're **pretending** and it won't be **real**.

or something.

You'll
regret
it
but not as much
as you thought you would.

Big
knickers
today;
thong
tomorrow.

Help is at hand,
but sadly it is help
from the
Elderly
Mad.

There is
no guarantee
and you left
the receipt
on the bus.

Oh,

poo parlour!

Things are deeply

UNFAB.

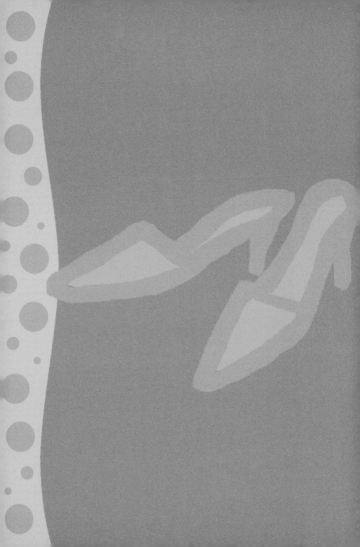

There is a
deeper
meaning
afoot.

It is something you **won't** forget – like **shaving off** one of your eyebrows or a bout of the **Cosmic Horn.**

Secrets are
secret
for a reason. Otherwise
they would just be
gossip.

Patience is a

virtue

but waiting is

boring.

You decide.
I'm in a hurry.
I can't be bothered.

Even though the

mangle

of love

lies ahead,

lead on.

Never trust a **chav** wearing slip-ons. **Or a chain.** Or trousers. Or a head.

Follow your
heart
to the Land
of the
snog.

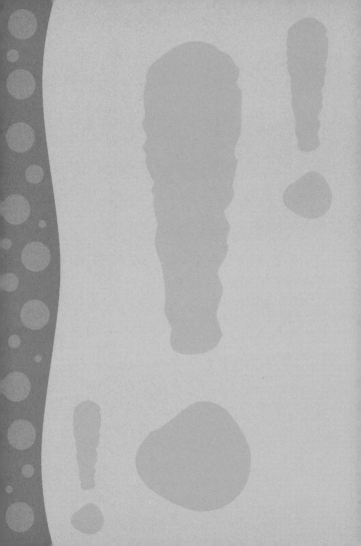

Prepare **to be startled!** Waaaaaaaaaah!

It is not that **you**
have put your
foot in it, more
that you have **danced**
up and down on it
as if you **need** the
piddly-diddly
department.

Better to have

snogged

and lost than never to have

snogged

at all.

By the time you count to a hundred in French, the phone will ring.

(If it is a French person put the phone down.)

Happy
days,
your
Sex God
has landed.

Strike

whilst the iron of
red-bottomosity
glows hot!

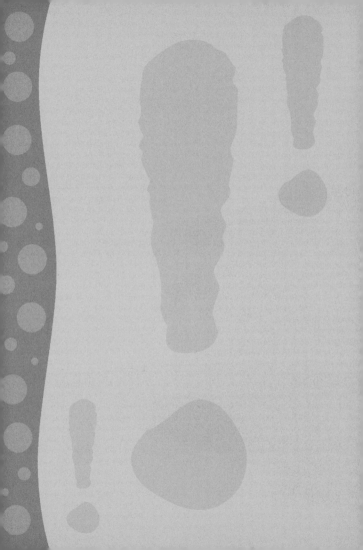

Erlack

and

pooey pongoes.

This is not

a good idea.

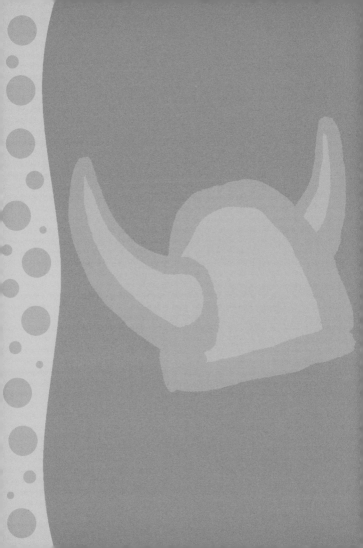

Stay level-headed. Nobody likes a lopsided girl.

Tomorrow is
a new day.
Unfortunately it
will also be
pants.

Take the
high road.
The low road
is clearly for the
tarty and
unfab.

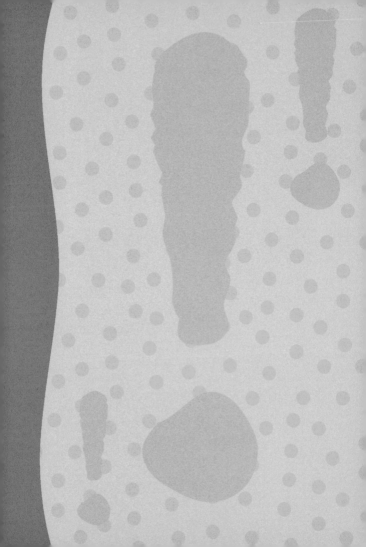

Who
do you think I am?
The all-seeing
eye?

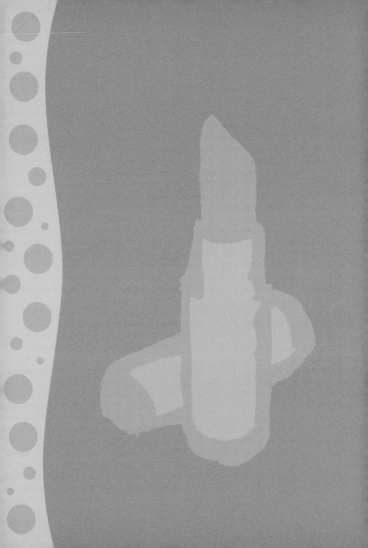

Flicky, Flicky, pout, pout.

You know it makes sense.

Snog on McDuff!

All you need are the
bare essentials:
boy
entrancers
and plenty of snacks.

You can take a
boy
to water
but you can't
make him
snog.

oo dgg
know? Mucho excitemond...
o be or not to be Ooooo-er Snog wisely W...
ygiddygodstrousers! Questions, questions, questions
I Know? Mucho excitemondo What in the name o...
To be or not to be Ooooo-er Snog wisely Wis...
ygiddygodstrousers! Fabbity-fab Questions, quest...
ow should I Know? Mucho excitemondo What in th...
ab To be or not to be Ooooo-er Snog wisely h...
ohmygiddygodstrousers! Questions, questions, questi...
hould I Know? Mucho excitemondo What in the nan...
-fab To be or not to be Ooooo-er Ohmygiddygo...
t in the name of PANTS? Ohmygiddygodstrousers
wisely Wisdomosity How should I Know? Mucho ex...
ions, questions Fabbity-fab To be or not to be o...
hat in the name of PANTS? Ohmygiddygodstrouse...
og wisely Wisdomosity How should I Know? Mucho ...
stions, questions Fabbity-fab To be or not to be...
What in the name of PANTS? Ohmygiddygodstrou...
Wisdomosity How should I Know? Much...
be or not to ...